Poetry Boys & the Poems They Left Behind

Wider Perspectives Publishing ¤ 2025 ¤ Hampton Roads, Va.

Copyright © November 2025, Destiny Nicholson, includes writing as Dezz
Wider Perspectives Publishing, Norfolk, Va
ISBN: 978-1-964531-20-5

Contents

I Took it Personal

Mirror, Mirror

I Took it Personal

Waterfalls

1. We broke up

2. Even after we broke up, we still fucked, as if the best place for you to hide, from the title you no longer wanted was between my legs

3. You used to get drunk on my smile. Tell me what it feels like to be sober now

4. I heard you found someone new to chase waterfalls with

5. I loved you the way the rocks love the waterfalls, prepared to smooth out all of my rough edges for you

6. You left me with memories, that eat away at me

7. Loving you is starting to hurt

8. Scars of the past are starting to burn

9. Teach me how to fall *out of love* the way that you did

10. No matter how hard I try I can't seem to **un**-love you

But none of these numbers should matter after 1.

4

Number 5

(after Daniel Garwood)

I loved you the way the rocks loved the waterfalls
Prepared to smooth out all of my rough edges for you
You,
Who never saw my efforts as love
Only obstacle

I was convinced
That love be work
That love be hard
That love be hurt

The last rock
Told you,
your touch wasn't enough to change her

Accustomed to your rocks turning into rolling stone
You crashed into me
And I be dam
For wanting you to stop running
You treated me the way you wished, you treated her
I treated you the way I wished, you treated me

I didn't want the change to happen rapidly
Just wanted there to be be evidence that I mattered
To you

That my love was enough to add something to you
You never let me add nothing to you
But were always content with taking parts of me

I loved you the way the rocks loved the waterfalls
Ready to protect you from anyone
Who stepped to you the wrong way

Prepared to damage souls for you
Didn't realize mine was included

I signed up to be scarred, you're right
After every collide
You would cool the burning
And I'd believe it was because you loved me

The reason these memories eat away at me is because
I'm not sure you did
You loved what you could get from me
Rock turned sponge
You squeezed out everything

Left me in need of therapy
'Cuz the world still sees you as waterfall
Beautiful, magnificent, force to be reckoned with
While I'm seen as weathered rock

If your claim is that love never lived here
It would explain why your waters
Were always so cold
And why I
Got stuck at number 5

Alternate Ending

It starts with hello.

      Ends, with I love you

Starts, with a smile.

      Ends with you being the reason

Starts, with me holding your hand.

      Ends, with you holding me

Starts, with a kiss.

      Ends, with forever

Alternate ending

It starts with hello, a smile, a hand hold and a kiss

Ends,   with you leaving

Dory

You must have forgotten you love me

Stop yelling at me
You're overreacting,
You're making a scene
It's not what you think

You must have forgotten you love me
I am not worthless
I have not lied to you,
I am not tryna fight,
Please, let go of my wrist.

See this is why I don't like to argue
Because you always forget

That you love me that is

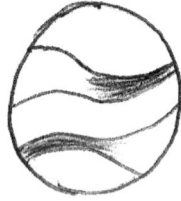

Planets Unaligned

I wanted us to live in Mars (Passion)
But seems you lived on Jupiter (Luck)
Putting in no work
I'm sure Saturn (Karma) has rings for you

We danced around Mercury (Communication)
Found ourselves lost in the moon (Emotions)
Venus (Love) was confused
We were calling Neptune (Illusion) her name

Strawberries
Orange juice
(concentrate)
Milk
Eggs
Chicken
Pizza (leftover)

Fridge

He told me I was sweet
Like strawberries
He's nothing like orange juice
Couldn't concentrate on me
Milking me for my naive nature
Like eggs that'll never become chickens
My dreams were bigger

Loving a man
Who treats me like the leftover pizza in the back of
The fridge

He knows it's not going anywhere
So it'll never be his first choice

Recipe for Heartbreak

(French Toast)

I haven't had French Toast since we broke up
Something about our spoiled batter
    Didn't make me eager to try a new one
Not sure what went wrong with ours

Did our vanilla not have enough French in it
When you extracted my Je t'aime et J'ai adore
It couldn't keep you from walking out the door

Was the griddle too hot to begin with
Causing it to cook unevenly
Could you no longer take the heat
So you got out the kitchen

Somewhere down the line
Taste buds shifted

Like we went from neutral to drive
Encountering clumps like our flour wasn't sifted
Was my heavy cream too heavy for you?

Could you not figure out how to mix our bickering
    With something sweet
Or leave it out of the recipe completely
Without leaving me out of the recipe completely

You, remind me of my grandmother
She too,
Had recipes she kept only on her heart strings

So I never go to read the instructions
Never got to be certain we were even on the same page
But still
I tried
To figure out what you might need next

Nutmeg, Cinnamon
    Maybe we can begin again

Pineapples, Strawberries
    It's not you, it's me

Powdered sugar, Whipped cream
    I'm still here, I'm still fighting

Syrup, Honey
    Don't throw it out, don't stop trying

I've seen you make French Toast
A thousand different ways
But you couldn't find a way to make this batch work
Tell me why didn't you want to make this batch work

I hear
You be in the kitchen with someone new now
While I
Still haven't had French Toast since we broke up

Lasagna

Loving him
Was a lot like loving lasagna
I love lasagna

But having to clean up the mess it makes
Is more pain than gain
More hard times
Than good times

And I am tired of scrubbing
Until my hands are raw
And my knuckles bleed

So, forgive me
If I finally decide to just throw away the dish
And not make it again

Dirty White Converse

(after Daniel Garwood)

You saw my shoes
And decided they told a story

Decided they told you everything
About who I am

Instead of where I'm from
Or what I've been through

You saw my story
And decided to play author

So...
Who was she?

The girl with the Dirty White Converse

And how bad did it hurt

Realizing you couldn't fix her?

You speak on traumas that have altered the sole
But I got flat feet and I'm a bit clumsy

So my sole needs more support

and my sides get scuffed

I will always trip over myself or walk through the

mud

Before I use you as a steppingstone

Who was she?
The one who used you as a steppingstone
The one who made you feel like
The Dirty White Converse
Were your fault
And your responsibility

The reason you now clean your shoes so meticulously

You no longer see beauty in the chaos
And can't fathom that someone can come to peace
With their dirt
Because you were never taught how to
Or that someone could still love you if you weren't
Pristine

I will not drag you through the mud
But understand you have to tend to the soil
In order for things to grow
So my shoes might be dirty

I will not ride until the wheels fall off
But I will help you change the tires
For us to keep going
So my shoes might be dirty

My aesthetic isn't "clean"
It's *authenticity*
So my shoes might be dirty

I am not a reflection of my shoes
I am a reflection of you
Tell me what you see

Chucks are not easy to keep clean
But they are not hard to clean
If you give a fuck
But if you want them spotless
Then you're looking for new ones
And I hope you find them

Mirror, Mirror

Poet to Poet

Poet to Poet
If we were a group
I could be your peace

I can hold you tight in my sonnets
You can wrap me up in your soliloquies
We can learn together what it is to take up space
When we get off stage

I'll be your mic
Personified
I'll be your speaker
Amplified
I'll be your stand
Won't let nothing slide
Teach you how to rest when your heart gets tired

'Cuz sometimes you gotta stop
Take a step back in order to propel forward

That's a poem
But a different poem
We are different poems
And together we could make a masterpiece

I've seen you beat bars into submission
Leaving the crowd beggin'
Master, please
You perform so masterly
But have you ever wondered what happens when two
masters meet?

Poet to Poet
I see us in movie magic
A few months turn into a lifetime
In the blink of an eye

This is not Beauty and the Beast
No putting a bow around neglect and calling it love
No story with plot holes
No Stockholm

More like Princess and the Frog
Tiana and Naveen type
Because we make each other look at the world
differently
Slime and mucus are not the same thing
And I want you in every one of my dreams

Digging a little deeper
Can be easier
When you have someone to feed your soul

Poet to Poet
I can read between your metaphors
Understand what you earned metals for
Promise I won't leave you asking what you met her for

I'll be the muse to you poetry
The Meg to your Hercules
I won't call it love
But I will call it inspiration
You can be the reason my pen move
And I'll be the reason you shake rooms
We'll be the 1 and the 2

Poet to Poet
If we were a group
Then I would be your peace

Reflection

They are poems left unfinished
Poems often forgotten
Usually the ones just left chillin'
In the back of that notebook
They are the mirror you avoid
'Cuz your reflection is too tough to face
They are more than a people
They are a place
Where love grows in spite of heartache
Where light shines anyway,

Mirror, mirror on the wall
I'm Sorry I haven't always been Kind to you
I forgive you for not always having been Kind to me
We were just collateral damage in each other's healing

Can I Be the Poem

For once
Can I be the poem

Can I be something you hold onto
Something that sparks such strong emotion,
You can't help but write it down
Or say it out loud
Truth be told   being the poet is exhausting

Poets love so deeply that it's talked about for centuries
Everyone wants to be loved by a poet
Not acknowledging that poets, too, need loving

This pen is heavy
To be a poet in love is agony
I'll notice everything

The slight change in your expression
Will cause a drastic change in my feelings

I'll notice the light leave your eyes before you do
When your touch is no longer warm
Your embrace no longer welcoming

And if we don't work
They'll ask for the poem
Before they'll ask how I'm doing

For once
Can I be the poem

I don't wanna breathe you into every sonnet
Instead let me be your breathe
Being up lifted with your every metaphor
While being reflected in your every simile
Staying engraved in your memory

Let me be something you write a poem about

Let me be your muse
My existence enough to spark creation
Even on chaos ridden days
I'll be the cause of something great

I'd much rather
Much rather
  Be the poem

So it's not my notebook pages who remember you
But yours who remember me
I'd be less likely to recall the hurt
If I didn't find it necessary to write a poem about it

I wouldn't have to throw out pens
 For still knowing your name
Cut sentences short
So my words won't paint an image of your face

You could be the love I take to the grave
Instead of the love I took to the stage

Just once
I want to be the poem

A poet's heartbreak is said to heal the world,
But a poem's heartbreak
Actually gets a chance to heal

How We Love

I loved him
The way I love Shrek

He loved me
The way he loves French Toast

But that's not his favorite movie
And I don't eat breakfast

Poetry

I will not stop reciting love poems that were written
about you.

Times are different
You are not mine
Nor I yours

But that doesn't change where those poems came from

It's like we were parents, them our children
They are the best parts of when we were an "Us"

There is love in those poems
The world needs to know a love so pure existed

Even if it was just for a moment

Extrovert

Self-doubt is my best friend
Crippling anxiety my friends with benefits
Depression that ex I just can't seem to rid myself of
Don't freak
Toxic relationships are Kinda my thing

I, have a habit of tripping over my insecurities
You can't see them, but they are always right in front
of me
They have a habit of finding it funny
To have my tongue participate in tying

So I hide
Where everyone can find me
Which means no one is looking

I hide in my extrovert
While my introvert is screaming

Landmine

Did you Know
That a landmine can stay active for decades
That it is only 7-10cm in diameter
And in order for you to activate it
You have to step on it directly

It happened so long ago
I thought the battle was over
But there are landmines in my fields of daisies
Convinced I was ready to bloom
Until he stepped the wrong way

Buried landmines
Blasting me back to when
I would pick shards of your ego out of my spirit
Like "you're insecurities are annoying"
Like "you hurt your own feelings"
Like "It's your fault, look what you made me do"
Memories I thought I pushed down deep

Buried landmines
Got me blowing up at someone who doesn't deserve it
My vision got blurry and I
Saw you
Heard you
Felt you

And now
He's picking pieces of who I used to be off his floor
Convinced that helping me through it
Is too much to ask of anyone
'Cuz It was too much to ask of you

Buried landmine
I lay here with silent tears
Like I'm used to
'Cuz "nobody's tryna hear all that" anyway
I isolate
Convinced no one will love me
When I have a chance of exploding

Buried landmine
No one ever asks the ticking time bomb if it wanted
this
Or how loud the tick is
Or even if it saw it coming
'Cuz I thought
I thought I was ready to bloom
Now I'm picking triggers like daisies

Some will say I'm wired this way
Forgetting I wasn't always

Buried landmine
Did you know
The one who created the landmine
Is rarely ever the one to turn it on
Or detonate it?

It's usually someone unexpecting
Sometimes it's someone who was just playing
Or walking the path they've taken everyday
But today
They stepped the wrong way

There are landmines
I won't discover for decades
But when they explode
I'll have to deal with the casualties

Buried landmines

My Love

(IZWAP)

If Zuko was a poet
He'd say how Fire bending, and poetry are the same
thing
If you only ever do it out of pain and anger
The skill disappears when you find peace

My love be Fire Bending
Be walking around with scars passed down by my
fathers ideals
Be holding my tongue as I get burned by relationships
I had no business being in

My love be shedding skins
Dawning new clothes to cover up old wounds
Unlearning toxic behaviors over tea

It be reconnecting with source
It be understanding my power, my capability
Be "just because this is all I know doesn't mean it's all
I'll ever know"
Be setting boundaries

My love be uncomfortable
As growth often is

Be asking questions
The Law of Attraction

Be fighting, for what I deserve
My love be Fire Bending
Because my heart
Be dragon

Dear Mr. Poet

Dear Mr. Poet
The bright lights look good on you
Love the way you give your all to a performance
No matter an audience of 50 or 2

But I can't help but wonder
Has anyone ever seen the poem in you

Noticed that the gold in your eyes shines nice and bright
When a bar hits the way you want it to
That there is intention in every one of your movements
You did this poem on purpose

Could they pick up on the disappointment in your tone
If you were to drop it?
Would they even notice?
'Cuz you know how to "keep going"
Perseverance looks sexy on you
Rest does, too

Mr. Poet
There are bags under your eyes
Probably 'cuz the perfect poem won't write itself
And when you're alone you try to edit yourself
The way you do your poetry
Meticulously

Mr. Poet
The safe places of the world are getting more scarce as
we speak
So I'm glad you found one in your pen

Becoming more comfortable
Being the center of attention
Kinda like you never got the chance to when you were
young

Speaking with the base in your voice
And having everyone listens
Kinda like you never got the chance to when you were
young

Being applauded
And reminded that you are enough
Kinda like you never got the chance to when you were
young

Mr. Poet
The stage feels different when you're on it
Like your inner child knows that he's safe here
Like your inner smile knows it has a place here
Like you know that you can put your armor down
For at least three minutes

The conversation you have with the audience is something
personal
And monumental

Dear Mr. poem
You hold more than the world will ever know
Not everyone can read between your lines

You are worth workshops
And ink stained note pads
Re-writes
And hand cramps

So if ever you need to break
    From all the things unwritten
Remember you are hangin' with people
    As indented by you as you are by them

And you don't need to break yourself
    To be something worth writing about

Colophon

Wider Perspectives Publishing regrets to have to announce that the ongoing Colophon page, used to tout artists published in books from WPP, has to be reworked. This is due to the **growing** library of fine writers coming out of, or even into, the Hampton Roads area of Virginia.

Ann Shalaski
Donna Burnett-Robinson
Arlandria Speaks (Faith Clay)
Faith May Griffin
Se'Mon-Michelle Rosser
Lisa M. Kendrick
Cassandra IsFree
Nich (Nicholis Williams)
Samantha Geovjian Clarke
Natalie Morison-Uzzle
Gus Woodward II
Patsy Bickerstaff
Edith Blake
Jack Cassada
Jada Lasha Hollingsworth
Daniel Garwood
Tabetha Moon House
Nick Marickovich
Grey Hues
Rivers Raye
Madeline Garcia
Chichi Iwuorie
Symay Rhodes
Tanya Cunningham (Scientific Eve)
Terra Leigh
Raymond M. Simmons
Samantha Borders-Shoemaker
Taz Weysweete'
Jade Leonard
Darean Polk
Bobby K. (The Poor Man's Poet)
J. Scott Wilson (Teech!)
Chris Green (thePoeticGenius)

Charles Wilson
Gloria Darlene Mann
Neil Spirtas
Jorge Mendez & JT Williams
Sarah Eileen Williams
Stephanie Diana (Noftz)
Shanya – Lady S.
Jason Brown (Drk Mtr)
Ken Sutton
Kailyn Rae Sasso
Crickyt J. Expression
Frantzy Civil
Ann Shalaski
Catherine TL Hodges
Crystal. Nolen
James Harry Wilson
Kent Knowlton
Linda Spence-Howard
Tony Broadway
Zach Crowe

Maria April C.
Mark Willoughby
Martina Champion
... and others to come soon.

the Hampton Roads
  Artistic Collective (757
  Perspectives) &
The Poet's Domain
are all WPP literary journals in cooperation with Scientific Eve or Live Wire Press

Check for those artists on FaceBook, Instagram, the Virginia Poetry Online channel on YouTube, and other social media.

www.ingramcontent.com/pod-product-compliance
Lightning Source LLC
Chambersburg PA
CBHW071358090426
42738CB00012B/3156